On The T

The Titfield Thunderbolt

by

Simon Castens

Thunderbolt Books

ISBN 0-9538771-0-8

First published 2000

Designed and typeset in Times New Roman by Thunderbolt Books.

Printed by the Omega Press, The Old Weighbridge, Newton St Loe, Bath

Acknowledgements

I would like to thank Peter and Ginny Barnfield for their proof-reading, advice and encouragement, my wife Lesley for putting up with the Titfield Thunderbolt in all its manifestations, Mervyn Halbrook for sharing his memories and photographs, Doug Smith for the generous provision of his photographs, and Julian Peters for giving me cheerful access to Ivo's wonderful photographs. I would also like to record especial thanks to Bernard and Jean King for their friendship, generosity and hospitality, all very much valued.

Photographs have been kindly provided by courtesy of the following: British Film Institute, Mervyn Halbrook, Bernard King, Julian Peters and Doug Smith.

Published by:
Thunderbolt Books
Brassknocker Basin, Monkton Combe
Bath. BA2 7JD
England

Thunderbolt@titfield.co.uk

Contents

Cover photograph:

Filming at Monkton Combe on Tuesday 24th June 1952. The Reverend Weech looks anxiously at his watch while boiler pressure rises in locomotive 1401 prior to taking the villagers' first departure from Titfield to Mallingford.

Preface

I have always been interested in railways and find maps and plans endlessly fascinating, being captivated by the ability of a simple piece of paper to create mental pictures of unknown landscapes.

After moving to Bath and a new school in 1970, one of many required purchases was an Ordnance Survey two and a half inch map of the city and its surroundings. Much more interesting than my suddenly comprehensive rugby kit, this map opened my eyes to a whole new world on my doorstep, including a "lost" station (Green Park), and an intriguing crossing of two railways at a place called Midford.

Shortly afterwards this last feature was brought vividly to life one evening in the school hall, when we were treated to a film which reputedly held some local railway interest - the "Titfield Thunderbolt".

At the time, the filming of the "Titfield Thunderbolt" and the subsequent closure of the Somerset and Dorset railway line seemed to be events in a pre-historic age to my thirteen year old mind - although in retrospect of course it was all recent history. My imagination was fired however, and through the school library and on my bicycle I had soon visited many places on the map and in the film, falling in love with the area and becoming truly "hooked" on local history in the process.

Since then much of what I found has gone, characters have passed away, clearly ballasted trackbeds have become hopelessly overgrown and England has moved even further away from the post war austerity and optimistic expectation which gave rise to British Railways and the "Titfield Thunderbolt".

Hence my reason for writing this guide, to record a piece of peculiarly English history and provide a key to a lost landscape still uniquely available to us through the "Titfield Thunderbolt" - I hope you enjoy it.

Simon Castens

Avoncliff, April 2000

Introduction

The "Titfield Thunderbolt" was made in the summer of 1952 by Ealing Studios, and was the first of their comedies to be filmed in "Technicolor". The screenplay was an original piece of work by T.E.B. "Tibby" Clarke, who was inspired to write the story after he was taken to see the Talyllyn Railway in North Wales by his friend the author Richard Hughes. The Talyllyn was the very first preserved railway in the World and had been taken over by enthusiasts in the previous year. Seeing a sign "Volunteer platelayers required" Clarke was struck with the possible comic consequences of the situation, and began to research and develop the story which became "The Titfield Thunderbolt".

Briefly, the film tells the story of how a group of villagers buys and takes over the running of their local branch line after it is closed by British Railways. After various failed sabotage attempts, the competing bus company "Pearce and Crump" eventually succeeds in wrecking the villagers' train, which jeopardises the future of the railway as a ministry inspector is due the next day. This leads to the ancient locomotive "Thunderbolt" being taken out of the museum and pressed into service, and the railway thereby wins the day.

Following a request to the British Railways Board by Ealing Studios for the loan of a suitable piece of railway upon which to make the film, the recently closed branch from Camerton to Limpley Stoke was chosen. The Mid Suffolk Light Railway from Haughley Junction to Laxfield was the other railway offered for the film makers use, but the Camerton branch was chosen because of the surrounding scenery, and the suitability of the local area to provide many of the required locations. At the same time as Ealing were looking over the Mid Suffolk Light Railway, it had inspired its own piece of fiction in the form of John Haddenham's *Love on a Branch Line*, and so it has also managed to live on as a work of fiction.

Unbeknown to Ealing the Camerton branch line had in fact been used for two earlier films, Gainsborough Pictures' "The Ghost Train" of 1931, and David Wainwright's "Kate Plus Ten" in 1938. In the "Ghost Train", a hugely successful stage play written by the Bath actor Arnold Ridley (Private Godfrey of "Dad's Army" fame), Camerton Station had become "Fal Vale", the mysterious junction station in which all the action takes place, whilst in "Kate Plus Ten", an Edgar Wallace thriller, Dunkerton Colliery sidings were used for some night scenes on a train. Interestingly, "The Ghost Train" was re-made some years later (1941) in a film featuring Arthur Askey, and it is this version which one sometimes sees on television - the "Camerton" version starred Cicely Courtneidge and Jack Hulbert, and one of the three reels of film has unfortunately been lost.

Locomotives and Railway Hardware

The brightest railway star in the film was undoubtedly *Thunderbolt* (real name *Lion*), a remarkable locomotive survivor from the earliest days of railways. Built in 1838 for the Liverpool and Manchester Railway by Todd Kitson and Laird, *Lion* was described on its order as a "luggage engine", and possessed an identical twin called *Tiger*. Other locomotives on the same order continued the wild animal theme, with two "coaching engines" named *Leopard* and *Panther*, and two "bank engines" called *Elephant* and *Buffalo*.

Nothing remarkable was recorded about these locomotives' railway service, but in 1859 the London and North Western Railway, by then the owners of the Liverpool and Manchester Railway and its locomotives, sold *Lion* to the newly formed Mersey Docks and Harbour Board for further use as a stationary boiler. Set up on blocks, with one axle removed and partially dismantled, *Lion* spent the next 70 years driving pumps at the Princes Graving Dock. Discovered by a writer for the *Locomotive* magazine in 1923, by which time her boiler had been disconnected, it was another four years before any action was taken to rescue this remarkable survival. In 1927, mindful of the forthcoming centenary of the Liverpool and Manchester railway, the Liverpool Engineering Society set up the "Old Locomotive Committee" and began to lobby for *Lion*'s preservation. They were successful, and in 1930 the Docks Board presented *Lion* to the society, and she was restored to as near as original condition as possible at Crewe Works by the London Midland and Scottish Railway, who were paid a little over £200 for the work.

For the centenary celebrations in the same year, Lion was set to work hauling visitors in a newly constructed "Old Time Train" around a specially laid track in Wavertree Playground. Once the celebrations were over, it was expected that *Lion* would be placed on permanent static display, and so it was that she was placed on a plinth on Liverpool Lime Street station.

Her retirement was not to be so restful as expected however, and after making an appearance in the 1937 film "Victoria The Great", in the following year she played a major part in the centenary celebrations for the London and Birmingham Railway. In 1951 she made another brief film appearance in Imperado Pictures' film "The Lady with the Lamp", a biography of Florence Nightingale, but in the following year achieved screen immortality in her starring role in "The Titfield Thunderbolt". A letter dated 14th May from Ealing Studios first requested her loan for the film, and following agreement *Lion* was used on location and in steam during June and July of 1952, during which time she performed reliably.

This historic locomotive still exists today and following an overhaul and several years in action during the Nineteen Eighties she has been retired again, and will be housed in the Transport Gallery of the Liverpool Museum. At the time of writing the museum is undergoing extensive refurbishment and whilst this work is being carried out, *Lion* has been moved to the Manchester Museum of Science and Industry where she is on public display for the duration of reconstruction works at Liverpool.

The two British Railways locomotives used in the film were ex Great Western "14XX" class 0-4-2 tank locomotives numbers 1401 and 1456, temporarily transferred to Westbury shed especially for the filming. Despite their old fashioned appearance, these locomotives were examples of a relatively modern class introduced by the GWR in 1932 for branch line traffic. No less than four examples of these locomotives still survive, and three of them are usually to be found working at preserved railways up and down the country.

The coach used in the pre-wreck train was quite unusual, being built for the Kelvedon and Tollesbury Railway and later used on the Wisbech and Upwell Tramway. At the time of the filming, this coach had been put aside for preservation by the British Transport Commission, but unfortunately it was later accidentally destroyed. The body of an identical vehicle can still be seen however at the Rutland Railway Museum.

Other stock seen in the film is a "Toad" Great Western Brake Van, (two were used, and many examples survive in preservation), a cattle truck, and Dan's house/coach. Although the latter was constructed by the studios, it is seen running on a Great Western "Loriot Y" truck built to carry steam shovels for working on the track. One of only two built, this last is possibly the only survivor from the film, (apart from "Lion") as one of these vehicles has been preserved on the Severn Valley railway. Two Great Western "Cartruck A" flat wagons were also used to mount the cameras on, but these are not visible in the film for obvious reasons.

Pearce and Crump's coach was a "Bedford OB", owned by and hired from Daniels' Garage in Winsley. Whilst many vehicles of this type survive in preservation, this particular coach is reputedly one of two such vehicles currently used for tours on the Isle of Man. It is difficult to confirm this however, as the coach was re-registered when it was taken to the island. Sid James' steamroller was a 1904 Aveling and Porter works number 5590, which belonged to Barnes Brothers in Trowbridge. Subsequently sold for preservation, this machine still exists and now belongs to an enthusiast near Swindon.

Shooting Titfield

The station that was immortalised as "Titfield" was Monkton Combe, a picturesque small station built by the Great Western Railway in 1910, and the first station along the branch towards Camerton from Limpley Stoke. The name "Titfield" was made up by Clarke, and is a simple combination of two place names, Limpsfield, where Clarke lived, and Titsey, a nearby village.

Filming took place at Monkton Combe and in the surrounding countryside for eight weeks during June and July of 1952, and hotels and guest houses were filled with film technicians, studio staff and film stars. The filming generated considerable interest in the area, and many local people were used as "extras" in the film, from Monkton Combe schoolboys to professional railwaymen. Whilst in the film the actors appear to drive the locomotives, three sets of locomotive crews from the Westbury locomotive depot of British Railways were actually responsible for driving the trains up and down the line. They were driver Bert Harris and his fireman Bert Stride, driver Sid Mitchell and his fireman George King, and driver Ted Burbidge and his fireman Frank Green. These last two are the crew which actually appear in the film as themselves driving the pre-wreck train, and together with Guard Harold Alford, who also appears in the film, they received screen credits for their appearance.

The first mention of the "Titfield Thunderbolt" in the local press was in the Bath Herald of Saturday 14th June, with the forthcoming filming achieving front page status. Technicians were obviously already in residence, being shown painting the new Titfield station sign, and it was reported that flower beds had been newly installed on the station platform and that a newly repainted coach was standing in the siding at Monkton Combe, awaiting a run down the branch in what would be the "first train on the line for two years". Harry Kratz, Ealing's unit production manager, was responsible for all work on the site for the Studios, liaising with Mr Leslie Edwards from British Railways, who was operations superintendent at Bristol. Bath Fire Brigade were also in attendance, being represented by chief officer W. Hall, and provided a trailer pump to supply water for the locomotives from a mill leat below the station.

Michael Balcon, the owner of the studios, and Charles Crichton, the director of the film, were due to visit Monkton Combe on Sunday 15th June, although in the event Balcon did not visit the proceedings. Instead Michael Truman, the producer, accompanied Charles Crichton and Douglas Slocombe, the cinematographer, on the first run down the branch from Limpley Stoke behind locomotive 1456. At this stage the Mallingford sequences were reported as being scheduled to take place at Weston super Mare, although in the event a part of Bristol Temple Meads was used.

Transported by low loading wagon from Liverpool, and arriving in Westbury on 13th June, *Lion* was driven under her own steam from Westbury to Limpley Stoke on Thursday 19th June. A special path was arranged, and *Lion* left Westbury at ten o'clock running light, and arrived at Limpley Stoke at five minutes past eleven, having travelled the ten miles at a restricted speed of 10 mph. One reason for the slow speed was that Lion's only brake was four wooden blocks acting on the tender wheels. This journey had taken place three days earlier than anticipated, as the locomotive had been found to be in perfect working order by the fitters at Westbury locomotive shed. After a pause, *Lion* was driven down to Monkton Combe and parked on the Mill siding, where the film technicians spent the next couple of days working on her appearance. *Lion* was repainted to better suit the Technicolor cameras used in the filming, with her livery becoming a bright nursery red and green, and acquiring various other embellishments such as a striking brass trim around her chimney stack and a new name *Thunderbolt*. When Bernard King, a film enthusiast who was visiting the set, asked Len Wills, the assistant art director, what *Lion*'s owners thought of her new paint scheme, he was surprised to hear the reply- "They don't know yet".

During the period of filming, *Lion* could regularly be seen out on the main line, and apart from her trips to Bradford Junction for turning she made weekly trips back to Westbury locomotive sheds for boiler washouts and maintenance checks. The veteran locomotive would invariably be saluted by the crews of passing trains, waving and blowing their whistles, and she made such a singular sight along her ten mile journey that many local people to this day retain clear memories of the locomotive passing by.

The well known local photographer Ivo Peters was also on hand to photograph the various comings and goings, and he recorded *Lion* parked on the mill siding at Monkton Combe on Saturday 21st June, and a few days later captured *Thunderbolt*, newly embellished and with the entire Ealing "train set" in tow on Wednesday 25th June.

The paper reported that Ealing expected to complete shooting the scenes at Monkton Combe station by Thursday 26th June, with filming then due to move to "Beal's Farm" followed by the village scenes using Freshford and finishing at Dunkerton colliery sidings, where the duel between Sid James' traction engine and the train was to be filmed. After this, *Lion* was to be taken to Bristol, where the Mallingford arrival scenes were to be filmed in the fish dock of Bristol Temple Meads station, before returning to Monkton Combe for her final scenes along the Camerton branch.

On Thursday 19th June, the day that *Lion* had travelled to Limpley Stoke, the film unit was at Winsley for the day, filming the scenes at Pearce and Crump's garage. Winsley's garage was used, belonging to Mr A H Daniels, who as mentioned earlier also provided the coach used by Pearce and Crump throughout the film. According to a report in a local paper, the day was quite cloudy, and most scenes were shot after 5 o'clock when the weather had brightened considerably. Stanley Holloway (Mr Valentine) had visited the filming during the day, travelling from his Combe Down guest house, but apparently had not been noticed by the fifty or so villagers watching the proceedings. This is just one example of the great care which Douglas Slocombe took with the lighting of the film, it at times caused apparent delay, but resulted in a film which is always superbly well lit.

At midday on Monday 21st July *Lion* was noted running through Bath at its customary ten miles per hour, being expected in Bristol over one hour later at around 1.30. The passage through Bath station was noiseless apart from the sound from the rhythmic swing of the coupling rods and an occasional puff of smoke being emitted from the three feet high chimney. Filming at Dunkerton had been completed on the same day, (this did not require *Lion*, as at this point in the story the more modern locomotive is still in use), and the Bristol scenes were due to be completed by Wednesday 23rd July- in the same week. Most of the unit was then due to return to Monkton Combe, and as veteran actor Sir Godfrey Tearle (Ollie Matthews, the Bishop of Welchester) had only arrived in Bath on Sunday 20th July, his scenes with *Lion* along the branch line still remained to be shot, as did the Titfield village scenes utilising Freshford village.

At this stage the location filming was almost finished and by mid August the film crew had gone, and things were nearly back to normal at Monkton Combe. The level crossing gates had been put back in to place, the additions had all been removed from the station building and the fixed "distant" signal for the junction with the main line had been painted back in to its proper colours. This signal, just on the station side of the old canal footbridge, had been disguised with green paint for the duration of the filming, as you can see if you look carefully in several shots along the station platform! Finally, on the 19th August, an 0-6-0 locomotive came into Monkton Combe station with about half a dozen low sided wagons and removed all the remaining film "props".

Although this marked the end of the location filming, there was still much work left to do in the studios. Studio work is generally carried out after location shooting, as the lighting can be more easily adjusted to match the location work than the other way around. Bernard King later picked up an amusing story from Ealing Studios art department about an aspect of the studio work. As it happens it involves the veteran actor Godfrey Tearle, in the scene where the two triumphant men of the cloth stand proudly on the footplate of *Lion* as they make their final run to Mallingford.

Using the full size replica of the locomotive, close ups of the two men were filmed in the studio against a photographically "trickled in" background of pleasant countryside speeding past. To add to the realism of this studio shot, pipes had been rigged up inside the replica's plastic boiler to supply steam to escape from the safety valves.

Unbeknown to the film crew however steam was also escaping inside the replica's boiler, and in the middle of a take it was noticed that the boiler's dome was beginning to sag as it succumbed to the build up of heat from the escaping steam. Large pieces of timber were hurriedly pushed up inside the dome to coax it back into shape before it set into its distorted shape.

Douglas Slocombe checks the Technicolor camera's view along the track.

Exploring the Landscape

For the purposes of describing the landmarks of the "Titfield Thunderbolt", I am going to take a journey from the eastern end of the film's landscape and work generally westwards. This is by no means the only way of actually touring the area on the ground, and if you want to explore all the locations mentioned in this description, then I think you will need more than one day.

Of course this will be especially true if you are tempted to sample the delights of the various hostelries that you will encounter on your journey, all of which offer potentially rewarding experiences. For what it is worth, I advise you to give in at least once on your journey - Titfield is a heady brew and ought not to be taken too quickly. In any event, you are unlikely to be disappointed, and who knows, you might even meet a film star.

So here's to our magnificent Generals, General Gordon and General Booth and all those who laboured to save the Titfield to Mallingford railway from obscurity all those years ago.......

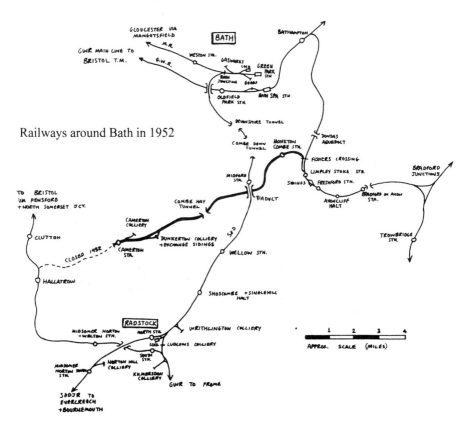

Railways around Bath in 1952

The Locations

Some of the locations described are on private land, and their description here does not imply any right of access. Most of the locations are viewable from public footpaths and roads, if you wish to enter upon private property to further explore then you should seek permission from the owners.

Freshford

Although Monkton Combe Station was used as Titfield Station throughout the film, most of the Titfield village scenes were actually shot in Freshford. The only part of Monkton Combe which appears in the film was Station Road, now called Mill Lane, on both sides of the railway (see later). Freshford was filmed from a point between the former Morris Stores and the Church in two directions, in addition to a view with the Squire and Rev. Weech in the actual churchyard itself - shot at five minutes past three according to the church clock. The house frontage of Morris Stores itself remains elusively out of view, but there are extremely clear and long shots down the road past the church towards the old brewery. With its elegant tapering Bath Stone chimney, this remains a distinctive landmark, despite some alterations to its windows since the film was made. It is down this hill that the red lorry is driven by Pearce, demonstrating to the Titfield inhabitants the dire consequences of "amateuritis".

In the opposite direction towards the bottom of the valley, there are several shots showing the population supposedly walking down the hill towards Titfield Station. In the film the next scene was invariably shot looking up Mill Lane in Monkton Combe, with the same population now walking towards the camera, but having been miraculously transplanted some four miles across the countryside. The illusion is very convincing, and is helped by the likeness of the two scenes, both roads have stone walls and similar architecture, all executed in the local Bath Stone. In this last scene, you will also notice that the intending passengers walk straight past an old fashioned direction sign with a black and white striped post, ironically this is the sign pointing the way to Freshford station.

A final scene which was shot at Freshford is that of Mr Valentine leaving his house to catch the first train. "Do you know what time it is? -Yes, summer double time my dear!" The house belonged to a Mrs Lane, and Mrs Valentine was played by Mrs Morris from Freshford. This house is down the hill from the church towards the brewery, but the garden has been altered to allow car parking since 1952, making identification somewhat difficult.

Limpley Stoke

Whilst Limpley Stoke Station does not feature in the film, the building is architecturally almost identical to Monkton Combe, the station which appears in the film as Titfield. The main difference is in the style of windows, those at Monkton Combe had fewer and larger panes of glass. In addition the layout was slightly different in that at Monkton Combe the "gents" was part of the main building. Apart from this, Limpley Stoke Station as it appears today is very much as was "Titfield" in the film; the method of construction, proportions and colours are just as they would have appeared at the time of filming. A good view of the station is obtained from the other side of the railway line, the Fordside tea gardens alongside the Kennet and Avon Canal providing an ideal vantage point.

Standing back beside Limpley Stoke station, take a look across the tracks towards the Avon Mill. Recently converted into offices for a computer software company, it has a surprising connection with the film.

An aspect of location filming is that "rushes" of previous day's filming need to be viewed at regular intervals, typically involving the use of a local cinema after its last showing - often a depressing prospect for all those involved. For the filming of the "Titfield Thunderbolt", Baynham Honri, Ealing Studios' technical supervisor, devised a unique solution to this problem with what he discovered at the Avon Mill.

Built as a wool mill, it had subsequently been used to process flour, rubber, and timber, but at the time of his visit was up for sale, complete with its three 60 year old turbines and functioning generator, all connected to a water wheel in the River Avon below.

A tenancy was hurriedly arranged, and a screen and projector were imported from Ealing studios and set up in the machine loft. The machine loft was at the top of the building, set above the 30 kW generator floor, which in turn was above the turbine room at river level. A projectionist, Peter Lacey, was brought out from Ealing studios, and he had the complicated job of hooking up all the equipment and operating the private theatre on water power alone. The grid through which the weir poured had to be kept clear of weeds, the turbines had to be fed with oil, and the generator had to generate. The power required by the projector's 25 amp 200 volt arc lamp had to be balanced, in order to "burn in" the lamp gradually at the commencement of projection, and Peter found that it took five domestic electric fires and a greenhouse heater to achieve this.

The entrance to the projection room was across a small wooden bridge to the station yard, and a small sign above the door proclaimed the name of the unusual enterprise - the "Hydrodeon". The door was in the gable end of the

Driver Bert Harris, fireman Bob Stride and the local shunter attend to *Lion* beside Limpley Stoke signal box on the day of her very first appearance in the area for filming, Thursday 19th June 1952. (Mervyn Halbrook)

Limpley Stoke Mill, temporarily re-named the "Hydrodeon" for Ealing Studios' use as a water powered cinema. Technician Peter Lacey stands to the left of director Charles Crichton talking to Cinematographer Douglas Slocombe, while to the right stands Gabrielle Brune with her white poodle. (Ealing Studios)

Pannier Tank no. 9612 heads a demolition train off Camerton Branch at Fishers Crossing on 15th February 1958. This is the location of *Lion* and her train on its final run to Mallingford as it joins the main line. In the background can be seen Dundas Aqueduct, also visible in the film. (Ivo Peters)

Preparing to shoot the scene in which the villagers survey their wrecked train, just East of Monkton Combe station. The use of filters gave the appearance of night-time in the film, note the dummy tree and green painted signal.

Director Charles Crichton, Cinematographer Douglas Slocombe and Camera operator Jeff Seaholme discuss their next shot at Monkton Combe level crossing on Friday 20th June. The retaining wall in the background is still standing today. (Bernard King)

Lion stands on the mill siding at Monkton Combe on 21st June. The wagon in the background is standing alongside the loading platform for the mill, and the GWR spear fencing to its left is still in situ today. (Ivo Peters)

Four days later on June 25th *Lion*, now suitably embellished for the cameras and masquerading as *Thunderbolt*, sets out from Monkton Combe station with the entire Ealing "Train Set" in tow. (Ivo Peters)

mill opposite Limpley Stoke station, but unfortunately you can no longer see it as a new extension has recently covered this part of the building.

A final claim to fame for Limpley Stoke is that the Avon Rubber Company started its operations in the Avon Mill before expanding into premises at nearby Bradford-on-Avon. The station here was also the junction for the Camerton branch line, the platform for which spanned the Winsley road alongside a third line of railway track. This span was removed in order to create extra headroom when double deck buses were introduced, but if you look at the abutments you can clearly see the extra masonry which supported the branch platform.

Winsley

If you turn right under this bridge and carry on up the hill and through Winsley, you can find the site of Pearce and Crump's garage, the village garage which belonged to a Mr Daniels. The garage has gone, but its site is marked by two very recently built houses on the south side of the road on the Bradford side of the village centre. Pass through the village, around all the sharp bends, and you will find the site immediately on your right as you breast the slight hill after passing the turning to Turleigh. The shot in the film is taken looking down this hill looking back towards Winsley village centre, and shows just how much the village has grown since the filming.

Brassknocker Bottom

Travelling back towards Brassknocker Basin, the next actual location is at Fishers Crossing, where a farm access crosses the railway just at the point that the Camerton branch diverges from the main line. The scene is where *Thunderbolt* and her improvised train carrying the ministry inspector join the main line, and are passed by an express train heading in the opposite direction. Standing on the opposite side of the tracks from the road, you have exactly the view of the camera, even down to seeing Dundas Aqueduct and the adjacent railway arch in the background. The actual tracks of the branch are long gone, but followed the line of dense scrub curving away from the railway line before running parallel to the main line and running to your left, back towards the junction at Limpley Stoke station.

The next location is just along the road where the branch crosses over the Cam brook on the two arch "Plaisters Bridge". During the race between Pearce and Crump's bus, in a shot supposedly taken from inside the bus, there is a clear view of the "enquiry special" train crossing this bridge towards Monkton Combe, the parapets being the signs to watch for on the film.

At this point in the valley, the film camera must have been placed at a considerable height to shoot the beginning of the race sequence mentioned above. In this scene, Pearce and Crump's bus crosses over the branch line on the Warminster road, and turns left towards the camera as the "enquiry special" train emerges from under the same bridge, and heads in the same direction. In reality, the train is heading away from Monkton Combe and approaching the exact spot as above - but in the opposite direction!

Brassknocker Hill

It is worth taking a bit of a diversion up Brassknocker Hill, past the Viaduct Inn towards Combe Down, as apart from being rewarded by splendid views in all directions, you will find a perfect photographic vantage point for one of the views in the film. This occurs at the small lay-by just before the road turns sharply towards the wooded area. Looking downhill and to your right you will see a splendid panorama of Monkton Combe and the Cam Valley beyond as far as the hills above Dunkerton. The course of the railway in Monkton Combe is clearly visible, the station site is marked by the raised sports pitch and the garden and house beyond this marks the course of the track bed beyond the station. This is the exact view that is shown from Pearce and Crump's coach on the morning after the destruction of the train and *Thunderbolt's* return to the tracks, the one which causes the crash with the police van.

At this point it is worth recording that one of the few locations used which was not in Somerset was Richmond Park. This was used extensively at two points in the film, in the sequence where the stolen train is driven across country ("Left for Titfield!"), and just after the above collision, when the police sergeant chases Vernon Crump across the grass - "I didn't do it!" - "What didn't you do?".

The "Clank"

The branch line from this point, by the entrance to "Brassknocker Basin", has been turned into a road to provide access to Monkton Combe Mill, which serves as a base for a variety of retail businesses. This part of the branch, known locally as the "Clank", after the name given to the railway by past generations of Monkton Combe schoolboys, features quite prominently in the film. Most notably this is as a background to the cricket match where the passing of the *Thunderbolt* and her train causes the batsman to be clean bowled, and from the track the same cricket pitch is today clearly visible.

Immaculately kept, the ground belongs to Monkton Combe School, although the players in the film were actually those of the Combe Down club. This part of the line also features at the point at which Dan and Mr Valentine set off on the pump truck to steal a replacement locomotive after the "proper" train is wrecked.

Also prominent in the film, as it is today, is Limpley Stoke Viaduct, an impressive solid structure built in the local Bath Stone to carry the Black Dog Turnpike Trust's road of 1846 from Warminster to Bath, and under which extend the playing fields of Monkton Combe School.

At the point in the cutting where a footpath crosses the old track is the site of a cast iron footbridge which had originally crossed the Coal Canal and which was re-used by the railway. Set upon high brick piers to clear the trains, it is visible in the background of a number of shots in the film. Although nothing remains of the bridge, part of one of the makers' plates is on display at Brassknocker Basin.

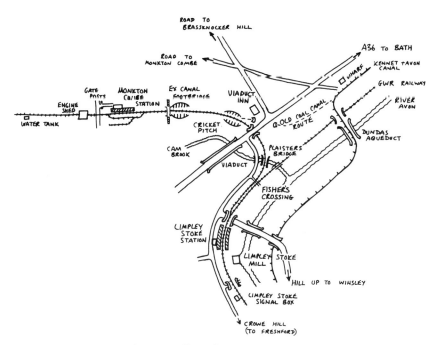

The Eastern end of the Camerton Branch

As you reach the very end of the track, straight ahead of you is a raised sports pitch, and this completely covers the site of Monkton Combe Station, blocking any further progress along the branch line. In actual fact, there is a little more to see at Monkton Combe, but you need to approach the site from the other end, by walking down Mill Lane to the site of the level crossing at the end of the station, which features in many shots during the film.

Monkton Combe Station

Having walked down Mill Lane, and past the old village "lock up", look to your left just before the change in levels which marks the site of the actual railway. The two black painted cast iron posts you can see on either side of recently constructed garages are the original gateposts to the road entrance to Monkton Combe station. It is through this entrance, embellished with an overhead nameboard, that Naunton Wayne sweeps on his bicycle to catch the train from Titfield. Further poking around on the ground will reveal the remains of the curved brick wall on which were set the iron railings of the station entrance, a detail which is also visible on the film if you watch carefully.

The level crossing gates here were removed by the film company, as they would have interfered with nearly all the shots required of the station, but were replaced after the filming was completed. For the same reason, the wooden hut which contained the levers which operated the loop points ("Monkton Combe West Ground Frame") was also removed, but this was not put back after filming finished, probably because it had been irretrievably demolished, but also because it was not required for any safety reason. The points would have been moved by hand during filming, and would have been secured in position by a padlocked clamp before any train was allowed to move over them.

Ealing Studios made considerable alterations to the station at Monkton Combe, extending the canopy and constructing a new external ticket window, and removing the screen from around the "gents" door on the end of the building, all of which features are clearly visible on the film. The station was also provided with numerous period details, such as weighing and chocolate machines. After filming was completed, all the extra details were removed and the building returned to its original state, lasting another six years until demolition in 1958. The station site lingered on for many more years before being obliterated by Monkton Combe School's new sports pitch in the early Seventies.

Whilst at Monkton Combe, it is worth relating a story about the scene near the beginning of the film where the Squire loads a pig onto the train at Titfield Station - the pig's name was Winifred. In 1952 there was an epedemic of foot and mouth disease, and emergency regulations put in place to contain this disease placed strict limits on the movements of livestock around the countryside. One of these limits lay between Winifred's pig sty and Monkton Combe station some fifty yards distant.

As this scene called for the movement of Winifred the pig between these two points, written applications were duly made to the Ministry of Agriculture. The reply came back that such movement could only take place "for the purposes of breeding". "Would the platform at Monkton Combe station be adequate for breeding?" asked the film makers, "It would" replied the Ministry, and so was this small bureaucratic hurdle overcome.

It may at first seem surprising, but all railway operations during filming were carried out under the supervision of a British Railways employee, under contract to the film company. Although Ealing Studios were only "playing trains", the potential dangers from their rather large train set were very real, and it must be a tribute to those involved that no major incident was recorded during filming. One minor incident was the "rather sharp pull up" sequence in the film, where *Lion* (*Thunderbolt*) is reunited with its train. The impact damaged the locomotive's framework, as the collision was rather more forceful than was intended, and actually features in the final film - watch how the tender moves vertically before the shot is hastily cut away.

Moving back to Monkton Combe, the engine shed which features in the film was placed over the running line on the opposite side of Mill Lane to the station, exactly as it appears in the finished film. What is less obvious from the film is that nearly all of the filming of the train required a departure through the engine shed! The shed itself was a metal "Dutch Barn", which despite the apparent ease with which the local population in the film carry it must not have been a mock up, but was a genuine article, permanently placed into position over the track. I say this because Bernard King took a photograph when he revisited the site a year after filming which shows not only the level crossing gates replaced and "in situ", but also all of the vertical uprights only of the engine shed still in place, but without any supporting roof structure!

The location of the engine shed is now part of the road which leads to the house and garden built over the trackbed, and the site has been further altered by the construction of another house on the opposite side of Mill Lane to the station entrance. This last change has made the greatest physical difference to the location, as it required the removal of quite a large piece of hillside, which from the railway's point of view was an allotment and fairly steep cutting, most clearly seen on film in the sequence where Emily tries to light the locomotive's fire.

The cottage which faces down the hill right next to the station entrance is still there, but since the film was made has had an extension added. With its roofline at right angles to the original structure, this unfortunately makes it rather hard to recognise what is a very prominent view in the film. Part of this cottage was borrowed by the film makers as a temporary cutting room, but unfortunately for would be film historians, all of the cuttings were put on the fire!

Before leaving Monkton Combe, there is one other little bit of the station which is worth looking at, even though it doesn't feature in the film. Walk a little way down Mill Lane, in the opposite direction to that which the Ministry inspector walks with Blakeworth prior to the final run, until the built up land which supported the station site is behind you. If you turn around, and look to your right, you will see that the original Great Western "spear" fencing is still standing on the very corner of the station site. The stone retaining wall to your right on which this fence stands supported the loading platform for the mill, which was next to the station siding and was connected to the mill by a wooden bridge, now gone.

It is difficult to believe, but this small platform and its connecting mill, was along with Monkton Combe School one of the very last customers of the railway. Known as "Freeman's Flock Mill" it used to manufacture furniture stuffing, and in its heyday even had railway wagons painted into its own livery. When *Lion* arrived, it was on this siding that the studio's artists altered her appearance, changing her name to *Thunderbolt* and embellishing her appearance to better suit the Technicolor cameras.

Between Monkton Combe and Midford

A great deal of the film was shot on this stretch of railway, views shown in the film are from both sides of the line, and tend to be taken looking down the valley towards the west. The water tank which features in the film was situated on this stretch of line, its approximate position was on the south side of the line, at the point where the garden along the trackbed finishes, and the disused trackbed commences. The farm from which water is collected is across the valley from the trackbed at this point, and is today called "Brett's Farm" - at the time of the filming it was known as "Dog Kennel Farm", and in the film it is called "Beal's Farm". I have found no trace of either the base of the water tank or the wooden bridge across the stream, although other visitors to the area have assured me that the base of the water tank is still there! This may well be the case as whilst the tank was a only a mock up, with its back wall cut down enabling a camera and operator to be positioned up there, it must have been a pretty substantial structure.

Midford

Midford is the second most used location in the film after Monkton Combe itself, for not only does it feature in the very opening sequence of the film, but the train is invariably shown passing under its viaduct on every journey it makes. This is a good point at which to note that the train travels indiscriminately in opposing directions on each of its screen journeys, which necessitated the locomotive's travelling to Bradford Junction, a triangular junction near Trowbridge, every time that it had to be turned around. The number of times that *Lion* made this journey is not recorded, but could have been minimised by shooting all the "westbound" and "eastbound" takes together. This problem need not have arisen with the more modern locomotives used in the beginning of the film, as two identical locomotives had been hired from British Railways, and their numbers were apparently swapped around, it is number 1401 that appears throughout the film.

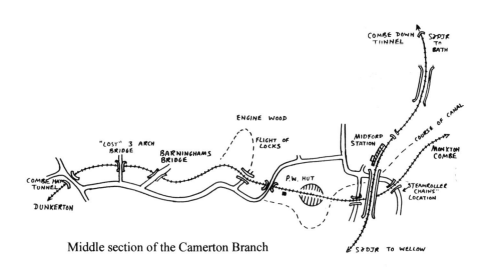

Middle section of the Camerton Branch

The railway which ran over Midford Viaduct was the "Somerset and Dorset", an important cross country link from Bath (Green Park) to Bournemouth. At its zenith in the 1920s, the S&D was a complete network of lines, with its own locomotive works and branches to Burnham, Wells and Bridgwater. The line eventually became a victim of the Beeching Closures which the "Titfield Thunderbolt" story pre-dated by over ten years, but unfortunately it escaped any form of preserved private operation, and closed to all traffic in 1966.

Whilst not strictly relevant to our story, it is a strange coincidence that Tibby Clarke, the writer of the Titfield Thunderbolt story, was a neighbour of Beeching's and used to travel into London with him on the train. Some years later he even got him to contribute a bit of dialogue for a film he was writing, Beeching providing some "technical gibberish" for a character in Benny Hill's first film "Who Done It?" - Beeching was a chemist at ICI at the time.

Midford viaduct is still very much in existence, and is a prominent and much loved landmark, a lofty and graceful structure especially when viewed from the minor road which runs alongside it. The opening sequence of the film shows a southbound train passing through Midford station and over the viaduct, headed by one of Bulleid's famous "West Country" pacifics, whilst the Titfield branch train passes underneath, heading eastwards towards Monkton Combe.

This sequence took several "takes" as both trains have to appear in the shot at the same time, and so the filming took place on a Sunday when there were no scheduled trains over the S&D for most of the day. For the record, the locomotive used was No. 34043 *Combe Martin*, and the Southern Region coaches hauled were typical of the local trains on the S&D between Bath and Templecombe at that time. The platform and foundations of the building at Midford station are still clearly visible, and are easily accessible through the car park of the "Hope and Anchor" pub, immediately adjacent to the northern end of the viaduct. From the vantage point of Midford station a good view can be had of the embankment and bridge abutments of the Camerton branch in the valley below.

Apart from the opening sequence described above, the most significant sequence filmed at Midford is that where Sid James donates his steering chains to the cause of the railway. The temporarily stranded train is standing on the embankment immediately to the north of the main road through Midford, and Sid James' steamroller is standing on the main road just below where the Camerton branch crosses it. As noted above, this location is clearly recognisable today, although the road is much busier than it was in 1952.

Looking north east across the platform of Monkton Combe station as modified by Ealing Studios to represent "Titfield", terminus of the branch line from Mallingford. (Douglas Smith)

A view of the modified station, looking along the approach road from Mill Lane. Both this and the above view were taken on a Sunday, probably early in July 1952, and there appears to be little activity. Note the ex-army radio transmitter, radio was used to control the movement of all trains during filming, the vehicle which hauled the transmitter is parked in the goods yard to the right of the picture. (Douglas Smith)

The villagers and Mr Valentine (Stanley Holloway) arrive at Titfield station for the first run of the train under private ownership. Note the heavy Technicolor camera and arc lights, the individual with the light cap below the camera in both views is Roy Gough, the Ealing Studios stills photographer. Sunday 22nd June 1952.
(both views Bernard King)

It's Thursday 26th June and the *Thunderbolt* stands alongside the water tank erected by Ealing Studios, just to the west of Monkton Combe station. Note the Bath fire brigade's pump by the stream used for supplying the tank with water, and the various lighting reflectors along the track. (Ivo Peters)

Ivo Peters' Bentley is parked alongside the line just east of the site of Dunkerton station, while the same demolition train as previously illustrated heads eastwards for the junction at Limpley Stoke on February 15th 1958. This is the location for part of the coach race sequence as described in the text. (Ivo Peters)

Filming at Bristol Temple Meads station, alias "Mallingford". Director Charles Crichton discusses the next shot with Producer Michael Truman (centre), and Art Director C.P. Norman (Ealing Studios)

The very last shot in the film. Whilst purporting to be "Mallingford", the scene was actually shot at Monkton Combe as this photograph shows - the whistle appears to be in working order! (Ealing Studios)

Before moving on from Midford, a final view which is worth watching out for occurs just after the scene where Joan empties the teapot out of Dan's coach and Crump says "might as well get out and push" - at which point of course the villagers are in fact pushing the train. If you look at the background as Joan sneaks out of the coach, what at first looks like a greenhouse is in fact the signal box of the S&D station, (the exact site of which is now the pub car park) and the whole of Midford station is then briefly visible before the camera cuts away. If you look very carefully in the background, you can see Midford's down starting signal, which the signalman "pulls off" for a southbound train from Bath whilst "in shot". This last detail is only really visible if you are watching the film on the large screen!

Between Midford and Dunkerton Colliery Sidings

The next location, which is used in several shots, is a gently curving stretch of low embankment which is filmed in both directions and from both sides of the track. The view which best places this location has *Lion* steaming along the embankment towards the camera and shows a hill and deep railway cutting in the middle distance. This cutting, the largest earthwork on the branch line, was about half a mile west of Midford, at a point where the Coal Canal follows the valley as it loops around to the south. The towpath of the old canal at this point is now a public footpath which runs from Midford as far west as Engine Wood, and is the best way of seeing this area as the road is out of sight some way to the north.

This location features several times in the film, and a little farther to the west, to the north of the third of three derelict locks on the coal canal, you can see the one surviving permanent way hut on the whole branch line. This is significant in as much as the roof of this hut can just be seen in the bottom left of the screen in the final run sequence, at the point where a woman and then other people run towards the train waving, just as the *Thunderbolt* leaves the shot to our left.

The hut owes its continued existence to the fact that it was used as a site office at the time that the railway was being used as a rubbish tip, even down to being equipped with its own telephone! This may seem surprising, but in the early seventies this old railway was one of the major tipping sites for Bath City Council, with much of Bath's rubbish being dumped along the line and in the large cutting mentioned above. The views of this stretch from the northern side of the line have been lost as the tipping extended to the adjoining field, on the north of the railway, to the extent that where the line was on a lowish embankment on its uphill side, it now runs against a cutting of rubbish, albeit disguised with topsoil.

Engine Wood

Rejoining the road at Engine Wood, you have arrived at another significant location in the film, although this fact may not be immediately apparent. You are standing where the old canal crossed the road, next to a lock keeper's cottage that has recently been extended out of all recognition and below a brick built bridge under the railway, which is at this point running along a high embankment. If you look west then you are looking down the road along which Pearce and Crump's coach was speeding in the final part of the "race" sequence, before it turned to your right, under the railway arch and came face to face with a car - "it's safer by road". This location takes a bit of believing, mainly due to the dense growth of trees along the railway embankment, but it is definitely the spot used. Incidentally, when you next look at the film, watch how the coach starts to brake as it enters the curve - obviously aware of the obstruction around the corner. The coach driver throughout the filming was Mr Roy Stokes, then an employee of A. H. Daniels, who was hired along with the coach for the duration of the filming. According to Roy, all of the coach driving was done at a slow speed, about ten to fifteen miles per hour, and then the film was speeded up to give the dramatic effect you see on the screen. Roy had to crouch down whilst driving, to keep out of sight of the camers, while the actor Ewan Roberts (Alec Pearce) sat on an orange box placed next to the drivers seat and pretended to drive the coach. Apart from the film work, the coach and Roy as its driver was also used by Ealing Studios to ferry the cast around Bath out to locations and back to their hotels!

Combe Hay

Travelling along the valley the next location is at the skew arched Barningham's bridge, which you will find by turning sharply right up a lane to a farm just before you get to the "Wheatsheaf" pub at Combe Hay. The scene here is where a group of children are seen running from one side of the bridge to the other and waving, as they watch *Thunderbolt* and its train pass by on its final and ultimately triumphant run. Although a lot of this cutting has been filled in, it is clear for a short distance either side of the bridge, allowing a good view of the attractive structure which is easily recognisable from its appearance in the film.

At this point in the film there is a view along the length of the cutting to a three arch bridge, and although the cutting is now filled in this bridge still exists, with just the parapets still being visible. Beyond this buried bridge the railway entered a cutting and turned to the south before eventually passing under the crossroads on the Wellow road in Combe Hay tunnel.

It was at the bridge mentioned above, according to an eyewitness to the filming in 1952, that one of the more modern locomotives was used to push *Thunderbolt* towards the camera before subsequently braking and hiding around the bend in the cutting. Apparently, this was a frequent practice during filming, as *Lion* could only reach a speed of 15mph under its own steam, and so the more modern locomotives were regularly used to propel the veteran into shot at speeds of up to nearly thirty mph! The film makers were not always entirely successful with this sort of ruse however, and in one shot of the train in Titfield station you can clearly see a plume of steam from an assisting locomotive in the distance.

Dunkerton

Several scenes are shot at the erstwhile Dunkerton station, mainly during the race sequence where the coach is running on a road behind and parallel to the train. Looking at the ground by the train you can make out the sleeper prints from a second track, this was the passing loop of the station which had been taken up in 1939. The trackbed at this point still exists, and is visible from the lane between Combe Hay and the main road at Dunkerton. Currently being used as a gallop for some horses, it is quite clear of vegetation and well defined.

Dunkerton Colliery Sidings

The broken down lorry sequence leading into the duel between Hawkins' steamroller and the train was shot at Dunkerton Colliery Sidings, confusingly named as it is situated some miles west of Dunkerton in the valley below the village of Carlingcott. This was the farthest point west on the branch line used, as far as I can tell, and it is also the most difficult to picture today. The reason for this is the extensive tipping which has taken place in the vicinity, completely obliterating this particular location. To make matters worse, the old Colliery, some buildings of which are still standing, has for some years been a scrapyard.

Broadly speaking, the railway ran in a fairly deep but wide cutting to the immediate north of the present day scrapyard, in which were extensive sidings built to serve the colliery. In the film, you can just make out the remains of additional tracks, and in one shot there are some old colliery buildings; the whole picture is confused however as the film company built a level crossing at this location.

The Western end of the Camerton Branch

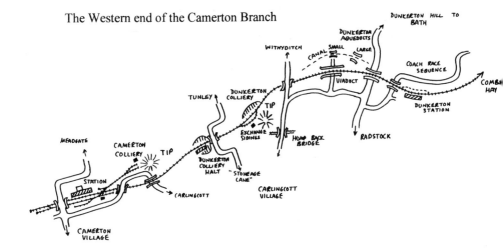

Dunkerton colliery, the development of which was one of the reasons for building the railway in the first place, had finally closed as early as 1927, and so was long derelict by the time that the film was made. The dirt batches still exist in large part, although if you climb up to the top, the "summit" is incredibly small, suggesting that some material has been taken away. I have heard a story that the tips were partially removed during the war, and the material used to construct Colerne airfield on the other side of Bath. The story came from a reliable local source and sounds entirely plausible, although I have not as yet seen any photographic or other evidence to support it.

The location within the colliery sidings site used for the filming was on the colliery siding track, just to the east of the site of the former signal box which had already been demolished at the time of filming. The ruined industrial building which you see in the background of one shot taken looking towards the locomotive is one of the colliery's winding engine houses. Looking at the OS map, this spot was in line with an angular kink in the northern boundary of the site, roughly corresponding with the western boundary of the colliery site. On the ground today, this equates to the marshy area at the eastern end of the private vineyard which occupies the site of the trackbed from the stone overbridge of Stoneage Lane, just near a row of tall Poplar trees. This should help you to locate the scene as a public footpath runs through the field just to the north of the whole site.

One film landmark in this sequence which is still clearly visible is the distant dirt batch of Camerton Colliery, which appears in the background of the shot of the lorry across the track as a starkly conical mound. Today it is the same size, although now covered in trees, and standing in the field to the north of the railway's route at the point mentioned above and looking west will give you a similar view.

Carlingcott

There is one much clearer minor location in this vicinity, which is where the lane along the edge of Dunkerton colliery's site crosses over the Cam brook on a hump backed bridge. This is the bridge over which the Squire drives his old Morris whilst trying to get past Hawkins' steam roller, and in fact the lane and a small gated entrance just towards Carlingcott were also filmed in this sequence, the entrance being where the Squire takes a short cut through a farmyard, although the farmyard is somewhere else altogether.

According to Vivienne Knight, Ealing's Publicity Director, John Gregson was not a car owner, and before the "Titfield Thunderbolt" had never driven a car. Apparently a "short but intensive training" enabled him to cope with the old Morris, but "modern automobiles remain(ed) a mystery to him". Quite ironic when you consider that he went straight from filming "Thunderbolt" to "Genevieve", where he was called upon to drive even more vintage machinery - and according to his daughter Mary, he didn't possess a driving licence during the making of either film!

Although the locations of these last described scenes are the farthest west down the branch line, the film-makers' trains would probably have travelled to the derelict station at Camerton to "run around", as there was no working loop at Dunkerton Colliery sidings. Camerton was by then the terminus of the line, although up until 1932 it had extended just over three miles farther to Hallatrow along the *original* branch, which was opened in 1882, see later for a fuller explanation.

Bristol Temple Meads

Of the locations which were not in the immediate vicinity, the most extensively filmed was Bristol Temple Meads which became "Mallingford" in the film, the main line station for the Titfield branch. The scenes were shot in the old fish dock, behind the present parcels platforms at the western end of the station. The cameras were placed on the southern side of the tracks and scenes shot in two directions, eastwards towards the distinctive overall roof of Temple Meads, and westwards towards the hillside rooftops of Totterdown and the iron bridge which carries the A4 across the railway. In all of these shots, you can clearly see the engine sheds across the tracks, and a wide variety of ex Great Western locomotives, with their distinctive copper capped chimneys.

To film these scenes, *Thunderbolt* travelled from Limpley Stoke to Bristol along the main line and was scheduled to spend three days filming there. During its journey it was restricted to a maximum speed of ten miles per hour, and it took an hour and a half to get from Bath to its destination, presumably spending quite a lot of time in sidings and loops to keep out of the way of faster trains.

Other Locations

The town through which the stolen British Railways locomotive drives along the road, supposedly Mallingford, is in fact Woodstock in Oxfordshire, and is clearly recognisable from the film if you visit the town today. The turntable from which the locomotive is stolen was at Oxford locomotive shed, and the open countryside into which it drives was Richmond Park, as mentioned earlier.

Finally, the scene where *Lion* is carried down the steps of the museum was shot at the entrance to The Imperial Institute in South Kensington, with the full size replica of *Lion* being used. Unbelievably, and amidst considerable controversy, this building was itself demolished in 1954 to make way for an extension to London University, although the tower from the original building was retained.

The Camerton Branch and the Coal Canal

The Coal Canal

The Coal Canal, opened throughout in 1805, connected the Kennet and Avon Canal at Dundas with the Somerset Coalfield by means of a route through Camerton to Paulton, together with a tramroad of 1815 from the canal at Midford to Radstock. Whilst the canal had been one of the most prosperous undertakings of its type, from the mid Nineteenth Century onwards it suffered increasingly from railway competition.

The first railway line to affect the Coal Canal was a mineral line from Frome to Radstock, which was opened in 1854 and extended to Bristol in 1873. This last extension passed close by the canal at Hallatrow, and several collieries defected from the canal to railway transport over this period.

In 1874 the Somerset and Dorset Railway eliminated all canal traffic from Radstock by opening its "Bath Extension" which was built on the route of the Radstock tramway, which the canal company had earlier sold to them.

The Camerton Branch of 1882 took even more trade away from the canal, and this coupled with the closure of a number of smaller collieries connected to the canal led to a further decline, eventually' leading to liquidation in 1893 and complete closure in 1898.

The route of the canal was eventually bought up by the Great Western Railway, who built the Camerton and Limpley Stoke railway along its length, which opened in 1910.

The Camerton and Limpley Stoke Railway

Opened in 1910 by the Great Western Railway, the Camerton branch of the "Titfield Thunderbolt" was primarily built to serve two collieries at Camerton and Dunkerton, and was an extension to an existing (1882) branch from Hallatrow to Camerton. The whole route followed that of the earlier Somerset Coal Canal, with the newer line actually utilising the canal's bed for much of its length.

Although the 1882 branch from Hallatrow only ran parallel to the canal for one and a half miles, it was the opening of this line that had finally put paid to the coal canal as a commercial concern.

There were a number of reasons why the Great Western extended the original Camerton branch eastwards along the line of the Coal Canal to Limpley Stoke, some more logical than others. In the first instance, a major source of traffic was available due to the proposed development of a large new colliery at Dunkerton, east of the existing line. Another consideration was that a large market for Somerset coal was for ships' bunkering on the South Coast -

Somerset coal apparently having good steam raising properties. This was relevant to the new line in that coal leaving through the Hallatrow line faced a circuitous route to its market via Bristol, and also a sharp gradient at the junction at Hallatrow which limited the size of trains that could be run. What was less logical was the element of competition introduced by a proposal for a railway into the Cam valley by the "North Somerset Light Railway", this company proposed a similarly routed line, terminating at nearby Priston, but which would connect with the competing Somerset and Dorset route at Midford.

It was this latter proposal which effectively forced the Great Western into building a seven mile long railway to full main line standards. Although only a single line, there were some major engineering and earthworks on the line, all of which were superbly engineered. In terms of load bearing structures and facilities offered, the new line could also take the heavier locomotives and boasted two fully equipped stations at Monkton Combe and Dunkerton, in addition to significant new sidings and works at the junction at Limpley Stoke.

Unfortunately the new branch did not live up to expectations, a major disappointment being the early failure of the massive new Dunkerton Colliery development which had completely shut by 1927. In addition to this, increased bus competition coupled with a temporary suspension of passenger services from 1915 until 1923 meant that passenger traffic was very sparse, and services were finally withdrawn in 1925. In 1930 coal from Priston colliery ceased to be loaded at Radford, along the original route, and in 1932 this part of the line was shut for good, and Camerton again became a terminus. Thereafter until closure in 1951, Camerton Colliery was easily the line's most important customer, and it was the closure of this mine in 1950 which ultimately sealed the railway's fate, the last train departing Monkton Combe on February 14th 1951. After the brief swan song in the "Titfield Thunderbolt", demolition commenced in November 1957, and was completed by December of 1958.

Screen People

Music **Auric, Georges** **1899-1983**
Made his composing debut at age 15 with a series of songs, going on to compose various instrumental pieces including work for the ballet and opera. Before the war he combined his composing with work as a music critic, writing for Paris Soir amongst others. Particularily involved with music for the cinema, including that on "Hue and Cry" for Ealing in 1947, he is credited with making a major contribution in this field.

Artwork **Bawden, Edward** **1903-1989**
English printmaker, graphic designer, illustrator and painter. After graduating he worked on a large number of projects for the Curwen Press, then many other publishers and also advertising work for companies including Shell-Mex and London Transport. During the War he was an Official Artist with the British Army travelling to Europe and the Middle East. His work has a simplicity of line and wit, although is generally not as naive as that carried out for the "Titfield Thunderbolt".

Coggett (Union spokesman) **Beckwith, Reginald** **1908-1965**
Chubby character actor, also writer of plays

Joan (Barmaid on train) **Brune, Gabrielle** **1912-?**
Born in Bournemouth, began career as chorus girl at eighteen, subsequently best known for review and cabaret work, screen debut in 1940 "Case of the Frightened Lady". Reputedly not very popular during filming of the "Titfield Thunderbolt", had high opinion of herself and took her poodle everywhere!

Screenwriter **Clarke, T E B** **1907-1985**
Journalist, well known in Fleet Street before the war, contributed a humorous feature in the "Evening News". Being unable to get into the Army he joined the police at the outbreak of war, and following discharge on health grounds, was introduced to Ealing as an advisor on pubs, having written a book about them. Michael Balcon gave him the opportunity to write scripts, thus starting his film career. His scripts were instrumental in defining the Ealing style, and he was unusual in making his name with original screenplays rather than adaptions, he was responsible for wroting most of the Ealing comedies. He receved an Academy award for best original screenplay for "The Lavender Hill Mob", and in the same year, an O.B.E. After leaving Ealing, his career faded somewhat, and he spent a lot of time following his interest of horse racing. Wrote autobiograpy in 1974 called "This is where I came in".

Director   **Crichton, Charles**   **1910-1999**
Oxford educated veteran of the British film industry, starting work in 1935 as an editor, and working from 1944 as director with "For Those in Peril" at Ealing. Directed most of the Ealing comedies. Was subsequently picked out by "Monty Python" team because of his work at Ealing for a spectacular return to films with "A Fish Called Wanda" in 1988, for which he received his first Oscar nomination.

Squire   **Gregson, John**   **1919-1975**
Scottish leading man, first screen appearance in 1948, went straight from shooting "Titfield Thunderbolt" to "Genevieve", several films subsequently, mainly action dramas and comedies.

Dan (Old engineman)   **Griffith, Hugh**   **1912-1980**
Flamboyant Welsh actor, formerly a bank clerk. Very many films , including "Ben Hur" in 1959 and "Oliver" in 1968.

Valentine (Financier of railway)   **Holloway, Stanley**   **1890-1982**
An outstanding and popular star of stage, screen and TV. Known for singing and monologues, he was a former music hall performer. Best known for his comedy characters, he was also a fine dramatic actor.

Editor   **Holt, Seth**   **1923-1971**
Began working for Strand Films in 1942 as assistant editor, moving as editor to Ealing in 1944 and working on many of the Ealing Comedies. His first moves into direction were unsuccessful, although he subsequently established himself in this capacity. His best known film is "The Nanny" with Bette Davis for Hammer films, and he was working on "Blood From the Mummies Tomb" when he died.

Hawkins (Steamroller driver)   **James, Sid**   **1913-1976**
South African comedy actor, best known for "Carry On" films and "Bless this House" on television. Died of a heart attack whilst on stage, generally keen on drink/gambling/women - latterly Barbara Windsor. He liked to maintain the story that he was a prizefighter and a diamond miner before coming to this country, in fact he was a hairdresser who got in to a lot of fights.

Emily (Weech's housekeeper)   **Martin, Edie**   **1880-1964**
Frail old lady in many films, on stage from 1886.

Vernon Crump (ticket collector)   **McGowran, Jack**   **1916-1973**
Irish character actor, last film "The Exorcist".

Reverend Weech   **Relph, George**   **1888-1960**

The son of an architect, originally to be a footballer for Newcastle, got consumption, went to South Africa to recuperate, returned to UK and then ran away from home to join Benson's theatrical company in 1905. Toured to New York and was picked out for films owing to his good looks, thereby becoming an early matinee idol in silent films pre-dating Hollywood. After volunteering for the army in the First World War, he was badly wounded on the side of his face, and subsequently didn't get any more film work for a long time. After some "character" roles in Edgar Wallace plays in the 30's, he became associated with Laurence Olivier and his Old Vic company. He then made a gradual move back into films in his later years. Father of the director/producer Michael Relph, also associated with Ealing, initially as an art director, producer at the time of "The Titfield Thunderbolt".

Alec Pearce (bus driver)   **Roberts, Ewan**   **1914-1983**

Scottish familiar faced character actor of stage, films and TV, appeared in many films up to 1982, including the "Day of the Triffids".

Cinematographer   **Slocombe, Douglas**   **1913-**

Started his career as a WW2 newsreel cameraman, particularly good at photographing period pieces, his style is credited with giving Ealing films their uniformity. After Ealing he has enjoyed a very successful career, directing photography on many well known films including "Jesus Christ Superstar" in 1973 and "Raiders of The Lost Ark" in 1981 for which he received an Oscar nomination.

Bishop   **Tearle, Sir Godfrey**   **1884-1953**

Distinguished stage actor, occasional films from 1906.

Ruddock (Conducts enquiry)   **Trubshawe, Michael**   **1905-1985**

Distinctive mustachioed character star of the '50s and '60s, a friend of David Niven and had been at Cambridge with Tibby Clarke.

Producer   **Truman, Michael**   **1916-1974**

Joined Ealing after being invalided out of the Army, initially working as a film editor. Subseqently worked with Michael Balcon after Ealing Studios were sold to the BBC.

Blakeworth (Town clerk)   **Wayne, Naunton**   **1901-1970**

A mild mannered light comedy actor, seen on the stage from 1920 and in films from 1931. Well known in films as comedy duo partner to Basil Radford, who had just died when this film was made.

Bibliography

Available at time of writing

Colliers Way	Peter Collier	Ex Libris
Country Railway Routes: Frome to Bristol	Mitchell & Smith	Middleton Press
Ealing Studios	Charles Barr	Cameron&Hollis
Sid James	Cliff Goodwin	Century
The Somersetshire Coal Canal, a pictorial journey	Halse & Castens	Millstream Books
Steam Around Bath	Ivo Peters	Millstream Books

Out of print at time of writing

The Camerton Branch	Maggs & Beale	Wild Swan
Forever Ealing	George Perry	Pavilion Books
A History of the Somerset Coalfield	Down & Warrington	David & Charles
A Lifetime in Films	Michael Balcon	Hutchinson
Lion	Adrian Jarvis	Liverpool Museum
Railways on the Screen	John Huntley	Ian Allan
The Somerset and Dorset at Midford	Mike Arlett	Millstream Books
The Somersetshire Coal Canal and Railways	Kenneth Clew	David & Charles
The Somersetshire Coal Canal Rediscovered	Niall Allsop	Millstream Books
This is Where I came in	T.E.B. Clarke	Michael Joseph

Recommended Maps for exploration of locations

Explorer map 155	Bath and Bristol	Ordnance Survey
Explorer map 142	Shepton Mallet & Mendips Hills East	Ordnance Survey

Appendix One

This has been reproduced before in books and articles which mention the film, and has been presented as a straight piece of writing by Clarke about his experiences in the making of the "Titfield Thunderbolt". In actual fact, it was a piece of publicity which Clarke wrote for a souvenir booklet produced by Ealing Studios for the premiere of the film, and so should be taken with a pinch of salt.....

It's Worse When you're Older, by T.E.B. Clarke, 1953

Never again will I smile unkindly at the plight of the man who catches mumps in his mid forties. Though personally I said goodbye to this complaint at the respectable age of seven, I had to wait until the 1950's to catch an even commoner childhood fever.

I had no ambition in early life to drive an engine - it never even occured to me to spot one. My father was allowed to play with my most expensive Christmas present unhampered by me. I regarded trains as smelly things liable to make one sick, their only virtue being the power they had to squash a halfpenny placed on the line into the size of a penny.

Came the dangerous forties and a visit to North Wales, where in the summer of 1951 I found myself standing on a station of the narrow gauge Tal-y-llyn Railway, blinking incredulously at a notice which said "Volunteer Platelayers Required". Curiosity had to be satisfied, and my inquiries brought the information that this was a private line run through the summer months by railway enthusiasts from all parts of the country, who spent their holidays as engine drivers, firemen, guards or booking clerks.

Thus was born the idea of The Titfield Thunderbolt: the idea of a village with sufficient love of its little branch line railway to buy it up and run it with an amateur staff when it came to suffer the fate of so many pleasant but uneconomic little branch lines in these materialistic times.

Two days of fact finding with the enthusiasts of the Tal-y-llyn line, and I had succumbed to the mania as completely as any clergyman in the land. Or perhaps you are not yet aware of the affinity that exists between the Cloth and the Boiler Suit? Almost my first discovery was the extraordinarily large number of parsons who are held in thrall by fascination with railways; it presented me with my leading character, the Reverend Samuel Weech.

The appearance of a few paragraphs in the newspapers about plans for this film brought a flood of helpful correspondence. "it occurs to me that you might like to make use of a delightful incident which took place some years ago on a small branch line..." Never was a writer so inundated with gloriously usable material.

Such enthusiasm is very infectious. By now I had developed and satisfied the long delayed ambtion to drive an engine, and it was becoming a question of whether my preoccupation with railway lore would make serious inroads on my work as a screenwriter. By this I do not mean to suggest that the railway enthusiast has no time for films. I asked one to make sure of that. "Oh I go quite a lot to the pictures", he said. "I saw Train of Events, Night Train to Munich, The Ghost Train, Oh Mr Porter....."

Well I finished my work on the The Titfield Thunderbolt last summer, and now that I have added to my record the supreme satisfaction of driving The Thunderbolt herself, I think I can safely say that the crisis is past and......

"Hullo! That you Clarke? Not too busy, I hope?"

"well I'm just writing something I've got to finish in time for...."

"Because I'm at Paddington - and what do you think I've just seen here? The new Gas Turbine - 18100."

"Not really? Oh I say! Wait for me - I'll be with you in twenty minutes."